The Apathy of Clouds

—

DOMENIC SCOPA

FUTURECYCLE PRESS

www.futurecycle.org

Cover artwork, a photocomposite by Diane Kistner from an original photograph by Isai Ramos; author photo by Alexis Groulx; cover and interior book design by Diane Kistner; Lato text and titling

Library of Congress Control Number: 2018946027

Published by FutureCycle Press
Athens, Georgia, USA

ISBN 978-1-942371-85-4

For Alexis Groulx

To err is human, to forgive, divine.

—Alexander Pope

Contents

—I—

Apple-Picking

In those days I thought their brief harvest
was the tremendous wheel that turned the seasons,
the years. On dirt trails that veined the groves,
I would see them fallen, red and green,
bruised as beaten flesh.

Every September weekend, suburban
to rural, my father drove the family to the orchard.
Excitement my alarm clock, I would spring awake
those frosty mornings. Most nights,
downpours drummed the roof,

my parents silent. For hours.
Even then I knew something of love
was callous, aloof. My mother always broke
the silence to read me bedtime stories,
the butterfly brooch my father pinned

to her sweater, tarnished, its wings pocked
with missing crystals. Wrinkles would crease
her forehead, relaxing slightly as she spoke
of goblins mining mountains,
able to swallow a child whole,

of princesses whose kisses could transform
toads to princes. The trance of apple groves
always glimmered through the gloomy forests of those tales.
Once, my father held my hand and pointed out
all the apples strewn throughout the unkempt grass

until I felt lost, lost among so much discarded fruit,
their hundred bodies spoiled beneath his boots.
That evening, after picking, he held me in the rocking chair,
football sportscasters a stable plot over the silence.

Fruit flies orbited the apple—marked with our mouths—
in his hand, his face floating over mine,
the house pregnant with tension,
delicate and dangerous as the human heart.

Posttraumatic

When I look at stars
I contemplate my father
snared by the seatbelt
in the ambulance he drove,
    and crashed,
watching his partner burn to death
in the passenger seat,
in a sea of flames
that recurs like the moon.
My father. Struggling.
To free himself.
Blood in his mouth.
The night, black
as charred skin.

He couldn't have predicted
the housing projects
my mother and I moved into
after the separation
or my back, lashed
with a calligraphy of scars
from the burning hands
of my abuser.

I was seven
when my father totaled
    the ambulance,
city lights dimming the brilliance
of dead stars trembling
in their bygone shining,
his partner cracked in half,
body curled
into that final position
burning things
so perfectly assume.

Cousin's Body

I never told this:
I saw my cousin's body twitch,
one last time,
before they covered it with a sheet,
crucifix nailed above his hospital bed
as if he had a final sin
to confess
before he reached the flames.
It was impossible
to watch him buckle up
for another fate,
another sky breathing solace,
or to see him wearing that white gown
as someone
being consoled or purified.

I was half-alarmed,
        half-ashamed,
to arrive so quickly
and witness him collapse
just minutes after the collision,
the snowflakes like confetti
in the scream of red and blue LEDs.
If only he could have read
the razor edge of that curve
        in the road
and the power of the plow,
droning with its diesel,
as it shoved snow
into his lane….

How hard it must be for poor Frankie,
        lost in mania
wherever he wanders,
the smell of gasoline still on him,

his wonderful eyes rig'd and relentless
as if locked in a debate
between the thrill of speeding
and the risk of arrest.
Anyone, even spirits,
could sympathize with his fierce decisions.
Worm-bound, faces decomposed,
    voices only dust,
they must nod to him and smile
in the silk darkness.

Study of a Mosquito

A mosquito cornered in the sun porch
in May
hankers for the heaven

of sodium streetlamps
beaming yellow,
like the bells of the jellyfish

hung in sun-starved waters
off the shoreline,
in a peace nothing disturbs.

Heaven must be there,
or it is nowhere.
Earlier, in the hospital lobby,

where there are always people,
they fed
or flew out slowly

to study prey
in the parking lot
murky with light,

their stings inescapable
as hypodermic needles
drawing blood all day and night

in some room in the cancer ward.
This mosquito's the shade
of soil after a downpour.

It buzzes back and forth,
as if claiming turf.
And its eyes,

when examined closely,
sheen without character
like oil slicks in sunshine.

It's been here a long time,
ticking against the screen door
and waiting.

It's midnight.
All the patients
are in their places.

Newlyweds in the Sarcophagus

Museum of Fine Arts, Boston, MA

When they found us in the gleaming vessel,
after we'd been cloaked in dry, straitjacket swirls of bandages,
it looked as if we were asleep.
Dreaming something. They left us like that,
not because of the serene, mocking shape
we formed in death. No.
It was because, by the time they found us,
we'd been spooning for centuries,
and when they tried, they couldn't separate us,
couldn't lay us flat and cross our arms across our chests,
as was customary, like the other corpses in the room
that looked like lonely lovers
struggling to stay warm.
They aren't lovers, but in death they are revived.
Even that was evident in the sterile, unrelenting light
and frequent shadows tour groups cast
as they roamed around
and we gazed out from the display,
the fingerprinted windows showcasing what was.
What was to come came closer
in a sudden clamor of conversations,
the glass confused with their reflections
as they gawked and snapped photos.

Observer Effect

on a hill overlooking a harbor

The startled dock
alive with them,
fishermen hosing
down their decks.
Spraying side-to-side,
they blast the scum,
attentive not to slip.
Surprise of foghorn.
Steadily aggressive
    hosing.
One just there,
on the bow,
disappears before
I take a breath
or can describe him.
No one moving
stays long enough.

How long
since we've worked together,
done anything together,
the way these fishermen work
their boat, washing,
making it
into a thriving thing.
Foghorn again.
I cannot catch a boat
in my imagination
on which I'd sail
with you.
In the slamming
of sharp sunrays,
a hose line
looks tangled;
the fisherman

seems snared,
kicking his foot frantically.
I haven't seen
the one
who was at the bow,
not for minutes.
Through a porthole,
two others
touch at their faces,
mouthing something.
Actually, they're eating—
I'm sick
of paying attention.

It's too hot
to swing here, in this park,
pushing off
with more momentum
to get a better look
at the boat.
Why bother
hosing down the deck,
why bother
leaving the bridge
for the bow,

why do I miss you now,
but not then,
the old you,
the you I molded
and remade
again and again,
until you hardened
into something else
entirely, more foreign
and untrue.

Why not look at seagulls
hurrying for scraps on the shore,
or across the harbor at islands,
or wonder why
that certain crowd
is spearing
sun-dried trash
on a far shoreline,
or if I'm capable
of recognizing you,
better or at all,
from this distance.

Man Painting a Fishing Shack on the Pier

There's the possibility, of course,
you'll plummet off the scaffold,
yet as always, as I walk here every morning,
I think of something else—
how lobsters navigate the mystifying forests of the seas
or how the water reflects the final strands of sunlight,
    reflects all that's left—
and I see the stubborn progress of your brush.
But I beg for you to keep in mind:
If you slip and plummet, swallowed
by the ocean's constant folding and unfolding,
I cannot hurl myself out there
to rescue you in swells like that.
Surely you can understand?
I can't be the fisherman to hook and pull you up,
drowned, covered in seaweed.
It can't be me searching in all directions for help,
alone, hearing the *shush* of high tide decompose
the pier's wooden support beams little by little,
the way, perhaps, downpours decomposed the swing set
in your backyard while your mother's voice called you in.

And if you do die, don't make me try to confess
what every moment of your life—
all the heartbeats, all the grinding forward,
inch by inch, of your body through every second—
signifies, when I'm only twenty-four, so overwhelmed,
like a sea lion plucking floating bits of food,
then suffocating with surprise
when the torpedo frame of a great white launches from below.
Do I really need to tell you why it all matters?
I mean, you'd be dead,
and a crowd would crane to see your corpse
rolling in the waves without breath,
which somehow escaped from you in all your carelessness.

Clearly, it would be cruel: You wouldn't be ready,
but would you recognize it works that way for everyone?
My being there would be cruel, too,
because of my unpreparedness, my shock,
my lack of anything to say except
you drowned, you drowned,
I didn't help, I didn't help.

Slave Trade Bracelet

Newport, Rhode Island

Those mansions we drove past, turning into shimmer in December
    sunlight,
those ancestral cemeteries, snow still perching on the tombstones,

the antique shops so small something was bound to shatter
if a boy, curious to touch the keepsakes, snatched a book out

from the bottom of a stack. In one of them
we noticed an old bracelet for sale that, although polished,

still seemed to hold shadows, especially in one dark spot
the seller must have missed, crafted with whatever

was available for metal in the nineteenth century,
bronze, or brass, perhaps. I'm not quite sure.

It reminded me of a shackle, of a slave trader
whose faith in the darkness of the world was stubborn

as a figurehead bracing against white-cap spray
as it slices to some port with a purpose no one mentions anymore.

Here now, he might as well have said when trading, *take this,*
as if in response to the wind, which was merciless—

Here now, he seemed to say to me as well,
Here's this metal. Where's my slave?

It made me wince to stare at it,
something familiar that tightened my throat.

It made me wince to see it sold there, too,
to say our trip itself, the mansions, each buff of the brush

to polish it under the poor light of some lamp
on a workbench, were tremendous privileges.

Because the slave traced for this bracelet is dead by now
and unknown, I think he had a scar, or birthmark, on his forehead—

I think he hated politics and fighting.
And if he outlived two bright sons, I think he still sang,

or hummed, out of hope or habit, songs in the field.
If singing is a salve, a bandage for despair, I think he could sing all day.

When I think of him, I think of that one small, unpolished spot
and traders, stubborn, believing in the darkness of the world.

How next winter, driving past this place—
which I've seen so many times and, often, in the worst weather,

when antiquated streetlamps make the snow seem whiter—
I'll shudder. And despite the ancestral cemeteries, stately with their
    history,

and despite the mansions abandoned to moonlight,
their luster scintillating solitary luxury, I won't be convinced.

Elegy for a Death in Utero

Before I crack open a beer,
my wife points out
the father digging holes
in the sand with his daughters,
how he starts to cough
and clutch his chest, twisted
    into suffering,
skin flushed and shocked.
I shouldn't stop to watch
toddlers splash each other,
or the leaden risk of storm
taking baby steps forward
    from the skyline,
until all wonder is erased.
His writhing freezes families
    under their umbrellas,
scared deaf
to my pleas
to call an ambulance.
When I reach him
through a current of panic,
he's not breathing—
      he's blue—
I can't stop shaking
to plant my palms
    on his chest,
which like a cedar barrel holds strong
until I start compressions....
But he's still the pale cobalt sheen
    of the suffocated,
and clouds have blurred the sun,
murky light swirling
    around us
as I attempt to jump

the motor of his body,
a cruel continuation
      of a stubborn will,
though I believe he'll die,
and I'll drown in my failure too,

until he swims back
and stares around the beach
as if in an afterlife,
his family only strangers
repeating his name
over and over,
their syllables gathering little
      of what's left
in the way of sunlight.

—II—

First-Time Flyer

A Boeing 747 Captain Roberts nicknamed "Buff." Flying, not as frightening as I had thought. But rather disheartening, touching, briefly, the souls of all those first-class transients, men and women I suspected were famous, successful. It was difficult not to admire them. They arrived, they conquered, they departed, and, like the crucifix of strobes blinking on the aircraft's underbelly, they were consistent. Their lives were like the slopes of straight lines on graphs or the trajectories of takeoffs: perfect.

And other people's lives? Nothing perfect about them. Let's say what's his name was born, his babysitter befriended him (closer than a babysitter should), he played street basketball with suburban kids (who called him bad words when he missed a foul shot and lost the game), he was lonely (then afraid), he loved freely, then not at all (then both at once), he graduated from a prep school (with average grades), he visited his dying grandmother (telling her his name repeatedly), she was watching a game show (he told her about the rape), knowing her mind would wipe out the fact, the way his teacher's hand erased the chalkboard after class…. It took them forever, all their lives, to reach that point. No way to be brief. No way to avoid baggage claim.

Occupy Prague

*June 2013, during a European study abroad touring
Nazi work camps, I joined fellow Suffolk University
students and participated in the Occupy Movement
in Prague. We slept in the camp with other
protesters, until we were eventually driven out by
police a few days later.*

They were what the native demonstrators named *budovy bastardu,*
    "skyscrapers of the bastards."
They were the shimmer and the distance.

We were the skeletal shadows of trees,
their cloak of darkness stretching over our tents
pitched haphazardly throughout the public park.

We circled the campfire at night,
but not to share scary stories.
We thought we knew what scary meant.
And we were never the stained-glass window panes
suffusing sacred spectrums inside St. Wenceslas Cathedral,
never the glint of light reflected off the golden chalice
lifted to the cross for transubstantiation.
We were the hollow clarity one notices in a wishing well
after a silver coin sinks below its surface,
the moment empty and clear as a beautiful god
someone has stripped nude of any power.

—

If police sirens and bullhorns possessed power,
we would have had, perhaps, a minute more
of some god's blessing to cease and scatter;
but that minute, blurring, became
only the rippling of reflections in wishing wells,
became only our lungs, worn out,
suspense and courage blending with every breath.

I could taste it for days, like the taste of budget wine
a priest swore was the blood of Jesus.
Jesus tasted like rust.
It freed my mind from my body, beaten with batons
so the bruises were the purple of a Lenten sash
left out on a sidewalk in the summer
to be trampled by pedestrians.
Left out why? For whom? For businessmen and beggars?
For skeptics and believers?
Who gives a shit on less than minimum wage?
We had left our bodies 'n that park—
within sight of the skyscrapers, the slum, the cathedral—
where diplomats could be seen walking
with security details toward the presidential palace,
where what was left of us
collapsed our tents, cleaned up our trash,
cried, embraced each other through it all, merging
deeper with this desperate company of justice and peace,
floundering like buffoons who hesitantly dig their pockets
for loose change to tip a hobo.

—

That rust we tasted on our breath was us,
that rust wasting away the benches we spray-painted.
And who knows whether those benches will rot into dust
or whether city workers will come and rip them down
to build new ones. It's a matter of perspective,
of how you see things there, now:
That crop circle of residual campfire,
the coffee can heaping with stubbed-out smokes,
blood-speckled grass, the booted warblers
      frightened into flight,
those children playing catch,
that beggar, that businessman, me, you.

Ghost of the Face Painter in the Park

Lhota Lake, Czech Republic

I am here. I've always been here,
sitting on the bench with paints and brushes,
in a small park blistering the pristine shore.
To be as learned as me,
you must ignore the slides and the swings—
their metallic coating patched with rust
from frequent summer showers—
and listen to the perfect language of seagulls
that know they'll not be caught stealing scraps of littered bread crusts.
You'll have to study how they scatter as if scared—
or out of some sense of, some means of, migration—
and smell the crack smoke as it's breathed out by the prostitute
who huddles underneath a cedar,
who bites her fingernails frantically before a shift
as she mumbles her apologies to a dead son.
Study the muscles in the calves of children playing football,
        scared by no one,
the offense congregating to devise a strategy.
The quarterback clenches his teeth:
He's going for a first-down.
Children used to wait in line here, impatient,
        for the face I'd paint.
The prostitute takes a hit off of the steel pipe
and watches them, watches the seagull wings like sails
casting shadows over the water, and the sand, and the swing set.
Today, as always, I predicted the hour of long shadows
and was wrong. Their shade means time for the children to leave.
They won't. They never do. And though they are the same children
who threw stones at the mother skunk swilling a tipped trash can
a week ago, and though they are so frightened
by the sweat of malice sheening their hands,
I almost feel sympathy for them, for this place.

Secretly, of course, I wish for them to learn a lesson,
a lesson so severe—that is to say,
a lesson only the ordinary world could teach.
As the end of summer hastens leaves from trees.
as this humid evening rots the eyes of the mother skunk,
I watch one boy cover a cough with his hand
and press his surprised thumb against a scar
that sparkles dull like a frozen lake he's never seen before.
The prostitute picking scabs
while manic molecules crank the engine of her heart
is too far gone to care.
She sprawls out on the grass
and lets the final beams of daylight nail her down
so the nerve-endings can learn what the sun can do.
The honesty of sunlight shows her every shame
and deems her body meaningless.

To become this learned, this powerless,
you'll have to sit with me for hours on this bench,
listening to the perfect language of seagulls,
watching this prostitute pray her mind will numb enough,
and then follow her into the parking lot
as she posts up underneath a streetlamp.
I can't help but stare at shadows
spreading throughout the park
and at the barren slide, refusing to succumb to rust,
and the swings lightly stirring in the breeze.

Swimming Pool

Terezín, Czech Republic

Past the gate where convoys spilled
their cargo of prisoners,
past concrete cells
too confined to sit down
and rooms where doctors
tried to calculate
the pinnacle of pain
the body could take
before it gave out,
past the double fences
where guards patrolled
    with Dobermans
for runners brave enough
to risk the wire's razor,
and past where the condemned concentrated
as the inmate band performed
on execution mornings,
there is a swimming pool
on the commandant's estate
    at Terezín.

Here the officers would congregate
for barbeques, hear the splash
of sunburnt children.
The commandant would coach
his son: *kick your feet,*
    turn your head to breathe,
would, every month, throw
a Jewish son and father
    into the pool,
saying to them, *whoever kills*
the other will live—
and toss them 2x4s.

Here his wife served
strychnine cookies
to the winner.

When the crematorium whistle
cried out and the sound
pelted tree leaves,
the children would dive
below the surface, touching
the bottom of the clear,
      soundless world.

Hot Peppers

a strip club in Prague, Czech Republic

After several shots my vision scans the bar mirror: attentive, beaming
lighthouse. High heels click. A stripper sits next to me. Strobes flare
up her platinum wig. On my thigh, her manicured fingernails trace figure
eights—*I bet you'd like to have your way with me, American?* My posture
stiffens tight as her corset. Newly single, needing time to mourn, I switch
the subject, brag I toured a Nazi work camp earlier that day for my study
abroad. *University?* she asks. *Then you learned about the Jewish son and
father forced to kill each other in the captain's pool, college boy?* Her English is
broken and sharp. I rise to exit. *I bet you didn't miss your shot to photograph
the gas chamber*, she says. My stool keels over. I stumble toward a set of
double doors. The bouncer cracks the granite profile of his face to wink:
She's a feisty one, American—his pupils constricted, his mustache clogged
with pilsner.

Tourists

on the train to Poland

Body stink saturates the train compartment. In the seat across,
Peter (German globetrotter I just met) forcefully takes my journal
when I didn't offer it and jots down a list of honey spirits to sample.
His dull pencil scribbles messily. I ask him to spell "Zytnia" several times,
his favorite Polish spirit. A woman aisle-struts, showcasing her red
sundress and aviator sunglasses, her lipstick tone like the one my Russian
tutor used to wear; her lips would pucker to accent all the syllables. The
railroad tracks gleam like a double-barreled shotgun. (My tutor told me
that her Jewish grandparents rode them in different cars). The train eases
to my stop, each wheel whining. (I wonder if her grandparents recognized
this shift in sound). Through the window, I spot a red cross spray-painted
on one of the station's brick walls, *GET OUT JEWS* in cursive beneath it.
Peter gives me back my journal and offers to shake hands, his hair blond in
the sun. With my tourist visa and journal, I feel my fist, imagine the bruise
on his face, and exit.

October Blues

Tonight, holding a hooker
    in my arms,
heat lightning,
cyclone-level tempests,
I think of you,
alone
or not alone,
in our distant hometown
during those last minutes
when the dive pubs
and the dance bars
with their sleazy clientele
are closing—
some strangers pairing off,
each desiring
what little numbness
the other offers….
Our clubs. Our hometown.
No.
Holding her, not you,
my clubs, *my* hometown.
Through a window,
I watch clouds
empty themselves.
I'll watch until the probing rays
of sunrise point out
the water-damaged ceiling,
point out the ripped-off blue dress,
the recycled syringes,
as if the sunlight could hold
    all things—
each piece of evidence—
to show me
or make me realize….

But it never manages to,
or it never tries hard enough.

All night I've slept,
    or not slept,
with some woman who
tomorrow
I will not want to see.
At least we'll never
have to deal with each other.
Soon, she'll migrate to another stranger—
I don't expect anything more.

Our hometown is so far away,
and I miss those moments
even though they were,
    most likely,
ordinary,
like any memories
hooked by human love—
the most relentless of barbs.

I remember,
after threatening your other man,
a mother blue jay building
her nest—twig by twig,
    fiber by fiber—
constructing it so solemnly,
as if it mattered...
sizing it up
    with such care.

Town Square, Krakow

When I make it to him,
strolling past
hand-sculpted mannequins suspended
behind storefront windows,
the overdosed homeless man
looks like a mystic dreaming
that his jar has grown full.
It takes only seconds,
seeing him there,
syringe still stuck
    in his forearm
and brown-bagged fifth of cognac
spilling its comfort
all over the cobblestone sidewalk,
to plunge back down the chasm
of my animal anger.
I'm sick of the drugs,
the addicts scrounging
on the corners of the seedy districts,
palms outstretched
as if to receive Eucharist,
the squalid sidewalks,
the fleshy pigeons refusing to fly.

I am sick
of the spirit of sympathy over everything,
that pleasure in sharing,
that religious understanding of pity.
I refuse to be moved by this addict's death...
and stare into his face
and walk away.
I am not going to stand
    in the frantic crowd,
with the rubberneckers

and self-proclaimed paramedics,
and celebrate the camaraderie
and silence
and lose myself
in the immortal tendency to cling.
Still, my hands are a little shaky
from his stiffness,
and my eyes have to blink away
the sight of his curved fingers
and unkempt beard,
his brown curls lifted by a breeze.

Rapsodia

a restaurant one block away from Auschwitz I

After savoring the first mouthful of smoked frankfurters—
    slathered with mustard and relish—
the man-at-the-bar's face shatters with ecstasy,
so eternal and frenzied it might be that of a homeless boy
just handed a bowl of flavorless stew at that shelter
    I crossed the street to evade.
A bowl of flavorless stew for a homeless boy, for his family,
for the expanse of souls that leered at me, one by one,
from hundreds of framed photographs
that lined the hallways of the buildings in the camp—
their imagined screams packing the atmosphere
to the hardness of a concrete slab. In the gas chamber,
the audience should have stopped chatting and snapping pictures
and been snared, slowly, like ancient creatures staring wide-eyed
at the randomness within the devastation of a comet's collision.
And now, here, I find myself towering with solitude,
repeating to this man's goddamned face:
Where is it, again? Where is it that you're from?

Little Consolation

*Loneliness is what happens at the end of any story,
including this one...*

—*Larry Levis*

The iridescent shimmer of an oil spill in the garage
is the scale of an angelfish.

Or is it the face of a girl,
the only high school dropout in her town,
after she decided to go through with the abortion?

Or is it sadness itself, sometimes difficult to see,
like the mirage of heat rising from the sidewalk—
there, if you look at it correctly,
then not there, then there again?

Or the place where little consolations,
like sunlight striking a loved one's pupil just right,

dilute?

And what can you do when the little consolations dissolve,
when you pull the blankets over your head
and only feel the heat from your breath?

Farewell

Krakow, absent or asleep
to other foreigners,
covered in stone, in ash,
who welcomed me,
I could not really escape you.
Even now I can't keep
from composing you,
cobblestone streets and buildings
and pale people.
I sleep to the sound
of your steeple bells that blast
at every hour.
I say there is no ghetto except
your ghetto, yet no trace of it
on the sidewalks near my hostel.
I dream of your clock tower ticking
        minutes, minutes
that cannot be stemmed,
of silvery storks above you
nesting in the rooftops.
Krakow, midnight moves on.
Here is the mead you brewed for me,
here is your currency,
no longer useful, pocket-wrinkled.

Here I am, having bathed,
        a bystander,
in the teargas smoke
of your gay rights protests,
in the sting and thrill
of them, the sharp scent
of their angers.

What was wrong with me?
Where was my flag,
my rainbow ribbon?
Krakow,
what ash, what stones
could I search behind?
I carried you a while
in my journals, believing
the memories would carry me back.

Krakow, I am still for you,
still a soreness, an ache for you.

—Ⅲ—

Walk-in Closet

I was seven—I knew nothing
of how he held my waist there

the way I hold my girlfriend's
as we make love.

     Her first time, she pleads, *Don't make me scream.*
I press her;
     Don't make it hurt so much!

Hurt as much
as I remember.

Seventh Birthday

What I remember is a worker falling
    off the roof,
muscled like my babysitter,
paint bucket slipping from his grip
that loosened as the ladder lost
its footing on uneven earth.

What I remember
is the smooth arc cerulean made
and the way its spill formed
an almost-question mark,
as if to mock the celebration.

—

Someday I'll return to the place
depicted by my memory, overgrown
with carpetweed and dandelions
and abandoned,
and through the chipped cerulean
I'll find the walk-in closet
with my rumpled clothes
and sit down, drinking nothing
but the stale air by the window,
and wait for my babysitter to finish
dressing, one leg, then the other,
and wait
until the atmosphere of the room
takes back the oxygen at sunrise,
and wait,
until each wrinkled crease
in the sweater and khakis
is as smooth as childhood,
    and wait.

At a certain time, that closet,
that room, that house,
will turn completely into light.

—

Because he told me to,
I pulled down my pants
and listened for the faint zipper
        on blue jeans,
and the possibility of *maybe not this time*
        already taking flight,
fickle, unaware, a hummingbird
launching off its branch
for another tree.
My hand hurried to strip the T-shirt
        to get there,
that moment of undoing.

—

The thunder of the worker's howl
and the complete uncertainty of cerulean
as it curved and shimmered in the light
and the inexplicable candor
        with which my babysitter
made his presence known
then wiped his body with a rag
were one:
the birthday, the nowhere, the nothing—
the perfectly baked cake
and the spilt paint's sprawl.

Stain

Let's start with this coffee I just spilled,
stain spreading, steadfast as the walnut floorboards
that must still swell with moisture
in the dining room,
window shades filtering the adamant,
decaying sun of summer evenings.
I focus all attention on the earthy, robust smell
that seems darker than the coffee,
and I refuse to recognize the way something dark
        and completely simple,
like this now half-cup of coffee, trembles
then stills a second as I hold it
and stare into it a long time,
until I am remembering that man
and how heavy he was the morning
he dropped from the South Tower,
and that house where I watched him on the television,
ten years old, with a certain sense, bewildering
and paralyzing as the takeoff of a plane is to a toddler.
And despite a looking back
that said goodbye before I could say anything
and his deep breath, his wave,
he still turned carefully away, forever,
scrutinized the skyline, face tilted upward
as if supported by the feeble sunrays
girdering through the smoke,
                and stepped off.
Sometimes, when I try to imagine myself as that man,
for seconds I feel released
and, if that release persists, terrified.
And, to be honest, as a child I was terrified of everything:
clowns, report cards, the filthy fingers of a family friend all over me.
But that other fear is different.

Even so, I thought I could forget that man
cascading through the chaos—determined, free—
and whether or not his fall was soothing.
Bathed in the television's tide of light, I sat,
a moth fixed to the flame of what it wanted,
and watched as the camera trembled,
        going out of focus....
Then came a reporter, sweat glistening on her forehead
as she talked,
the microphone shaking in her hands.
And all the youth I felt,
whatever left me in my nervous laugh,
did not return in the deep breath I drew in
        slowly, a second later,
the first breath of a young man.
And who knows where that boy went,
too numb to speak about what he *thought*
was only someone's cowardly surrender.
But maybe, after all, he's here,
in this coffee stain on the carpet—
its shape not a body flattened on concrete,
but only the random result of gravity,
a blind design with a silence and force
that transforms everything.

Sanctuary

Wolf Hollow, Ipswich, MA

Bored with dehydrated beef the conservationist throws to him, the alpha-male Argus—who lost his sole love when she snapped her leg—wanders the fenced-in pasture and its amnesia. It seems that mourning compels him to shuttle past the cave mouth, back and forth, back and forth, a dark dweller, like the train that crosses the horizon, transporting teenagers to the Halloween carnival four towns away so budding couples, arm in arm, can test their boundaries of trust on roller coasters. There is no station here, but the train whistles like held breath escaping, or the tenacious squeak of a hinge on a steel gate that swings shut and can be opened no more. When his brother, Grendel, earning the etymology, tried to claw the way to alpha, sadness weak in any species, staff banished Argus to his own caged paradise stocked with plunders of deer carcasses, lemongrass, bilberries…. There, he waits for her to reappear with the rest of the pack, each pup growing greater. The train passes. Argus lies down. His body shudders, doesn't sleep. Before a bone ripped through the flesh and fur of the mate he chose for life, I would watch him nuzzle his nose into her neck, the two of them running side by side, as if to race away from our world.

Luck

I'd rather not say
why it means so much
to me to watch

freshly hatched
sea turtles scramble
sand dunes,

struggling ike
toddlers w th missing
letter blocks trying

to spell g-d's name,
their flipper tracks
a sand-script—

lemon-spotted domes
immediately beautiful
to stalking seagulls

that swarm
the sky,
rushing down,

flipping shel s
to devour the underbellies.
A few survivers

reach the surf,
coconut husks,
captives to the tide.

The Apathy of Clouds

Sundown, sky
the shade of barreled bourbon.
My body stays inside.
I study its movement
and plan my tricks,
sunshine playing hide-and-seek
beneath the shoulders of trees.
Tonight my loneliness will vanish,
      a magician's trick.
I hear, outside,
the sound of trapped bees
buzzing on the sill,
a couple speaking reconciliation,
the creepy *breep-breep-breep*
of the crickets orchestrating
pleasure in the suburb.

—

      Just now,
I noticed my mouth,
how it speaks, without permission,
its preferences for prostitutes
and college sophomores
or for simply shutting down
like fluorescent signs
closing strip joints.
Right now, it brags
like a bulky jock.
I recognize, briefly,
reflected in her eyes—
two blisters bloodshot with tequila—
that already my face is clay
sculpted into whatever it takes
to completely have her,

cheeks sex-flushed
the crimson of a clown.

Outside, even the aureole of the moon
     is ashamed
and covers up its light.

—

One night all the laughter,
all the Cuba Libres on the house,
     dried up.
So I got lost
in bars,
on cabaret dance floors,
and hung my head
the way a dog does when it's left behind
until I was alone
as an orphan of the state.

Then something funny happened.
On the walk home,
waiting to cross the street,
a starling's shit rained down
     like shrapnel
and struck my shoulder.
I carry trauma,
and the world consoles
with its radiating stench.

—

Once I thought my lust
was someone else's will
that interfered,
like radio static wiping out
     a favorite song.
So I shut up
and sulked my college campus

like the troubled teen who sprayed
armor-piercing rounds
into his science classmates
        last semester.
I sat through the static.
Then I bared my teeth—
        I rose—
I screamed out like a blind man
falling through a lake's frozen surface,
for no reason at all,
reaching out for you….

—

Our conversation cracked and broke
like the top layer of snow
after a night of bitter cold.
And there was only the slam of a door
        as you walked out,
blunt as a hung-up telephone.

Outside in snowfall,
the spruces whitened hastily
and pinecones dropped in the drafts.
Addiction my ass—
        and, just like that,
your love was snuffed out,
hovering close to the ceiling.

—

I think I have control now,
as a mugger, desperate for a meal,
stalks the corner and listens
for the click of someone's heels
and a deserted dog howls
through missing slats
where the fence meets the sidewalk.

Lighting a cigarette, I squint
smoke out of my eyes
as the traffic signal turns,
and a driver floors an SUV
like a felon on the run.

I inhale through it all,
      deeply separate.

—

After half an hour my lungs surrender
to the memory of being a little boy,
      raped without a sound.
And I don't hear anything
as I try to leave the flesh behind
and open out
like a skydiver,
my arms and legs spreading
beyond their limits,
as the apathy of clouds and wind
      cuts through me.

In the Land of Fields

The final time my babysitter sinned
was when he mapped a way
and made forgiveness possible
for how his hips slammed into me.
If I could do it, he might also,
someday, wherever he strayed,
be so humble to forgive himself.

—

Wanting solitude,
longing for the simple loneliness of travel,
I said farewell and flew to Poland.
Descending, I looked down
at snow powdering fields
and small towns,
each house with a steeple roof—
and then the scowling tarmac,
thump of touchdown....
Then nothing.
Still he followed,
and every woman I held close
felt like my captive.
Run away. Or don't.
Most of my decisions have seemed wrong.

—

Once, at dusk, I strolled
the foggy streets of Warsaw,
the pavement puddled
and reflecting,
and at that hour, alone,
I stopped hearing the sigh of traffic,
discussions, the racket
of winter wind lifting leaves
high above the sidewalk lamps.

When I heard my nephew was born,
I thought how noisy
this world must be for him,
how mortal.
That night, to spite a missing person,
I refused to listen
to the sound of cathedral bells.
To be honest, I was still attached.
My babysitter died and I was still attached.
It seems so strange to say it
quite like that—
but how else can I say it?

—

When I wake up,
I confront the mirror,
press the safety razor to my skin.
I uproot a breath.
My body craves to hold
and to be held.
Because there are faces
I may never see again,
I must say
there are two things about darkness
and what it does to us:
Her bright, hooker eyes
when I flicked the light switch off,
how the pupils constricted
as if in blind faith,

and my babysitter closing
the closet door,
shadowed and speechless.

Notes

"Apple-Picking" borrows "delicate and dangerous as the human heart" from the poem "Insect Life in Florida" by Lynda Hull.

"First-Time Flyer" owes a lot to the poem "Brief Lives" by Jim Moore.

"Swimming Pool" is in response to, and owes a lot to, the poem "The Swimming Pool at Villa Grimaldi" by Martín Espada.

"Tourists" borrows "like a double-barreled shotgun" from the poem "Terminal Days at Beverly Farms" by Robert Lowell.

"Town Square, Prague" owes a lot to the poem "Behaving like a Jew" by Gerald Stern.

"Seventh Birthday," "October Storm," "The Apathy of Clouds," and "Ghost of the Face Painter in the Park" owe a lot to the structure and style of poetry by Larry Levis.

Acknowledgments

Grateful acknowledgement is made to the following publications in which many of these poems first appeared, sometimes in different forms: *Aji, Apple Valley Review, apt, Belleville Park Pages, Bombay Review, Borderlands: Texas Poetry Review, Boston Thought, Caliope, Cardinal Sins, Coe Review, Contemporary American Voices, Diverse Voices Quarterly, FLARE: The Flagler Review, Gravel, Grey Sparrow, Literature Today, Malpais Review, Misfit Magazine, Niche, Poetry Quarterly, Red Earth Review, Reed Magazine, Reunion: the Dallas Review, The Bayou Review, The Grief Diaries, The Mas Tequila Review, The Missing Slate, The West Trade Review, The Writing Disorder, Tule Review, Two Cities Review, Two Thirds North*, and *Visions International*.

Grateful acknowledgement is also made to the One Fund Foundation at Suffolk University, which awarded me the 2014 Robert K. Johnson Poetry Prize and 2014 Garvin Tate Merit Scholarship.

I would also like to thank the following people for their special assistance and support: Ralph Angel, Matthew Dickman, David Ferry, Jody Gladding, Thomas Christopher Greene, George Kalogeris, Fred Marchant, Tracie Morris, Betsy Sholl, Leslie Ullman, Robert Vivian and David Wojahn. Additionally, I would like to thank my family: James Scopa, Gerrie Scopa, and Alex Scopa. Of course, this project would have been impossible without the endless love and support from my partner, Alexis Groulx.

About FutureCycle Press

FutureCycle Press is dedicated to publishing lasting English-language poetry books, chapbooks, and anthologies in both print-on-demand and Kindle ebook formats. Founded in 2007 by long-time independent editor/publishers and partners Diane Kistner and Robert S. King, the press incorporated as a nonprofit in 2012. A number of our editors are distinguished poets and writers in their own right, and we have been actively involved in the small press movement going back to the early seventies.

The FutureCycle Poetry Book Prize and honorarium is awarded annually for the best full-length volume of poetry we publish in a calendar year. Introduced in 2013, our Good Works projects are anthologies devoted to issues of universal significance, with all proceeds donated to a related worthy cause. Our Selected Poems series highlights contemporary poets with a substantial body of work to their credit; with this series we strive to resurrect work that has had limited distribution and is now out of print.

We are dedicated to giving all of the authors we publish the care their work deserves, making our catalog of titles the most diverse and distinguished it can be, and paying forward any earnings to fund more great books.

We've learned a few things about independent publishing over the years. We've also evolved a unique, resilient publishing model that allows us to focus mainly on vetting and preserving for posterity poetry collections of exceptional quality without becoming overwhelmed with bookkeeping and mailing, fundraising activities, or taxing editorial and production "bubbles." To find out more about what we are doing, come see us at www.futurecycle.org.

The FutureCycle Poetry Book Prize

All full-length volumes of poetry published by FutureCycle Press in a given calendar year are considered for the annual FutureCycle Poetry Book Prize. This allows us to consider each submission on its own merits, outside of the context of a contest. Too, the judges see the finished book, which will have benefitted from the beautiful book design and strong editorial gloss we are famous for.

The book ranked the best in judging is announced as the prize-winner in the subsequent year. There is no fixed monetary award; instead, the winning poet receives an honorarium of 20% of the total net royalties from all poetry books and chapbooks the press sold online in the year the winning book was published. The winner is also accorded the honor of being on the panel of judges for the next year's competition; all judges receive copies of all contending books to keep for their personal library.

www.ingramcontent.com/pod-product-compliance
Lightning Source LLC
Chambersburg PA
CBHW070012100426
42741CB00012B/3211